The Great Le

Contributors from the Everything Indie Over 40 online community

Edited by John Hartley

The Great Leap Forward
Copyright © 2019 i40Publishing
All rights reserved.
First paperback edition printed 2019 in the United Kingdom
A catalogue record for this book is available from the British Library.
ISBN: 978-1-913218-53-9

No part of this book shall be reproduced or transmitted in any form or by any means, electronic or mechanical, including photocopying, recording, or by any information retrieval system without written permission of the publisher.

Published by i40 Publishing

For more copies of this book, please email: i40publishing.gmail.com

Printed in Great Britain by Biddles Books Ltd, Kings Lynn, Norfolk
Cover design by Ruby Hartley

Although every precaution has been taken in the preparation of this book, the publisher and author assume no responsibility for errors or omissions. Neither is any liability assumed for damages resulting from the use of this information contained herein.

The photos are from the personal archives of the contributors and may not be reproduced without express permission of the respective contributor.

The Great Leap Forward

Contents

Introduction (contributors: *John Hartley, Alex Towle*)

It Began On Radio (contributors: *Paul Bennett, Dermot Greene, William McAlpine*)

Fabulous Friend (contributors: *Ian Fergie, Tracey Bowen, Alisdair Smith*)

Running Order Squabble Fest (contributors: *Peter Fraser, Jon Peachey*)

Kill Your Television (contributors: *Simon Smith, Neil Budd, Nicola Tyzack, Paul Asplin, Ben Vendetta*)

A Trip Out (contributors: *Adele Pascale, Mark Whitworth*)

Sleeping With The N.M.E. (contributors: *Russell Barker, Rob Morgan*)

Outro

Title credits

------ Introduction ------

In the beginning was *The Word*.

Before that, there was *The Chart Show*, and long before that *Top Of The Pops*. Before music television there was music in print – New Musical Express, Melody Maker, Record Mirror. And before that... well, we just had to rely on word of mouth to hear about good music. Everything has a beginning; what makes the introduction to 'indie' so important is that 'indie' wasn't ever just about music. It was about a way of life. It was about that feeling, often awoken in early teen years, of being different from the crowd, of an alternative line of thought, taste in clothes, belief systems even.

'Indie' has never been just about a record on an independent label – Kylie and Jason could both claim that yet neither would be viewed as anything other than popularly commercial. And as Barry Lazell notes in 'Indie Hits 1980-1989', the Stiff record label is "historically regarded as a seminal independent success story", yet qualifies the absence of their catalogue from the indie charts on account of being pressed and shipped around the country with substantial assistance from major labels. There's nothing wrong with the mainstream, of course; it just isn't... well, *us*.

Instead, indie has been more about a more leftfield train of thought, the embracing of the unusual, the 1980s rarity of a vegetarian in the family, the person with coloured hair with clothes that couldn't be bought on the high street. Stereotypes, it is true, but still helpful in defining the vague entity of 'indie'. In his book 'How Soon Is Now' Richard King notes the "catch-all" nature of the term 'indie', continuing "An 'indie' band's songs document their passage into adulthood with the odd jarring chord sequence [and] a sense that no-one has been through this sort of thing before"[1]. This captures the essence of stories contained here, as the various contributors make their own passage into adulthood with the accompanying joy at the discovery of something they didn't realise existed.

We all have a beginning and are all, by and large, channelled into social norms by school, family, media and commerce. There's thousands of opportunities for sociological theses within that one sentence, but that is not what this book is about. Rather, it is about celebrating those second beginnings, those new starts, that great leap forward when people first formally

---

[1] How Soon is Now, Richard King, Faber and Faber 2012

embraced the change in culture that would come to define their adult lives.

These are moments so precise, so special, so individual, and yet every one of us can relate to them. They are our stories, the events that channelled our lives away from the mainstream: Take for example Alex Towle, who owes his lifelong love of alternative music to a combination of football and father:

> The summer of 1996. My dad was a big music fan; I always remember him having a lot of records stacked up in his back room. He picked me up one Saturday – the day of England versus Spain in the quarter finals of the Euros. I'd been following the tournament and me and my dad were watching this match together. With my pocket money I'd bought 'Football's Coming Home' on CD by the Lightning Seeds with Baddiel and Skinner and took it round my dad's. We listened to it. My dad wasn't too impressed; he put on 'World In Motion' by New Order. I can remember thinking, "This is fucking ace!" He could see I liked it and followed it up with 'State Of The Nation'. That was it. I was hooked.

A similar mix of father and football provided my own first forays into independence. I can remember how, if not exactly when … One Wednesday evening early in 1988, my dad picked me up from a Bolton Wanderers reserve match. It was the first team's first ever season in the Fourth Division. I was 15 and thus eligible for a child rate season ticket (£25 for the season, standing in the Burnden paddock, with free admission to reserve matches to be viewed from the relative luxury of the Manchester Road stand) yet old enough to go to matches without parental supervision. Night games were great, especially as Bolton were on a roll and actually winning games. In winter though the late journey home could prove to be a bit of a challenge, especially if I just missed one of the half-hourly buses from the Moor Lane bus station to Westhoughton. Dad occasionally offered/agreed to pick me up from one of the railway bridges in our new car: a 'W' registered, third or fourth hand Vauxhall Cavalier. We didn't have a telephone yet, and colour television was only just making its way into our living room, and this was the first car we had owned as a family since 1979 when poverty knocked upon our door and relegated my sister and me to a childhood of public transport.

The green tinge of the Burnden Park floodlights would still illuminate my walk to the railway bridge half a mile away from the Normid Superstore that had eaten into half of the north end of Bolton's ground, and into the car I would climb and retune the radio (a bonus!: the car had a radio!) from dad's preferred BBC Radio 2 to Radio 1, where as far as I was concerned there would be more interesting music to be heard. At this point in time my record collection included most of The Beatles' albums (on cassette), several singles by Nik Kershaw, the odd one here or there by Paul Young and Phil Collins, and some (what I would now deem) terrible middle-of-the-road singles by acts like Mr Mister, Kenny Loggins and Boris Gardener.

And then, that mid-winter evening as we drove down amber-illuminated streets I heard a song that was ultimately to change my life. This probably sounds dramatic, and maybe to some it would be an exaggeration, but I know different. The song had the catchiest chorus I had heard for a long time, the guitars chimed and reminisced about the 1960s, and the band had a name that was unforgettable. So when I awoke the next morning, why could I not for the life of me remember it?

Possibly because I was being numbed by the music that was in the charts at this time and dominating the airwaves. The dregs of Tuesday lunchtimes at school would invariably involve a cluster of boys' heads gathered around a small and tinny radio being hidden from the view of any passing teacher under old-fashioned wooden desks, as we listened to the announcement of the new Number 1 in the Top 40. This was a diversion from the usual lunchtime practice of becoming as sweaty as possible chasing a football in the concrete-floored and steel girder-ceilinged school basement. Contenders for that coveted chart-topping spot at this time included Bros with 'Drop the Boy', Climie Fisher with 'Love Changes Everything' and Debbie Gibson's 'Only In My Dreams'.

On Tuesday 1st March 1988 the single at the top of the UK charts was soapstar-turned-popstar Kylie Minogue. The song was 'I Should Be So Lucky'. Prophetic, maybe ... the evening of this particular date brought with it a visit to see Bolton Wanderers' 2-0 home victory against Tranmere Rovers, a win which would take them up to third in the division, the last automatic promotion slot. The journey home that evening in that rusting Cavalier brought further good fortune, and this time, there was no way I would be forgetting the name of that band.

The Mighty Lemon Drops would grant me an unexpected kudos and cement my membership of the circle of people who became my closest school friends. There were not many people at school with whom I could relate. School was generally not an especially pleasurable experience for this working-class-rooted teenager. Social stigma prevailed amongst the rich and wealthy who dominated the classrooms and there would be an equal mix of horror and mirth when I had to put down the telephone number of my granddad, living five miles away from me, when the football squad were gathering contact information for summer training sessions at the end of my second year there. It was a struggle to befriend people who lived in what appeared to be completely different worlds to me.

I shared little in music with my friends; our mutual interest was often football. But music was quick to take over from football as the dominant theme of pleasure in my life, especially when Bolton's promotion from the fourth division in 1988 led to little better than an embarrassing 2-4 early season home reverse against local rivals Bury. At that point, I gave up on football.

It is at this point that the subject of Physics joins the story, in perhaps the one single instance of my entire life that the subject has had even the remotest impact. This particular morning, tired of a non-working electrical experiment involving batteries and light bulbs (didn't all Physics experiments involve batteries and light bulbs?) the group of friends with whom I played football at lunchtimes surrounded the pencil case belonging to Hurst. Previously, his 'Winnie the Pooh' pencil case had been redecorated to portray the bear as a stubbled, monocled, tattooed, stick-wielding character. On this occasion people were writing obscure band names on the pencil case. I knew they were obscure band names because when I asked the reply came: "They're bands. You won't know them." I didn't. Undeterred, I made my contribution: The Mighty Lemon Drops.

"The Mighty Lemon Drops? You've never heard of them!" came the half-scornful dismissal, forgetting that obviously I had heard of them, otherwise I wouldn't know to write their name down.

"Yes I have," came my equally half-scornful reply. "They've got a single called 'Inside Out' and my mum's buying it for me today. And I'll bring it in to prove it!"

This changed things drastically, and I was – for the first time in my school life – slightly popular: inundated with requests to borrow it. (If you will allow me to stretch the term 'inundated' to mean five or six.) However, our teacher brought the proceedings to a quick end; too much noise meant we had obviously managed to get our circuits working. They most probably weren't ...

Having remembered that band name when I awoke the morning following the Bolton match, I had insisted that my mother should take advantage of her weekly Wednesday off work and head into Bolton. This was a trip she was planning to make in any case, of that I have no doubts, and there she would be able to buy for me the single I had heard on the radio the previous evening. I would pay her back, of course, and by the way it was called 'Inside Out'. This task my mum obligingly and dutifully agreed to fulfil, possibly worn down by previous teen-hormone-driven pleas for the purchase of goods (by way of example: a particular type of shoe, which all the popular boys at school wore and which I convinced myself would be the one thing to persuade the girls to find me attractive. The shoes weren't, and the girls didn't).

Unfortunately, on my return from school the following day I was confronted with the news that mother had been unable to purchase the single. Fortunately, it appeared that the band had just released an album, which was all the HMV staff could locate within their store, and mum had bought that instead. On tape: handy for the Walkman, and handy for sharing.

For both Alex and myself, these fiercely remembered moments in time capture points in which our lives would change course forever, when the faint rays of identity began to seep over the horizon: our indie beginnings.

John Hartley, Editor.

------ It Began On Radio ------

For many of us for whom alternative music provided the spark to help pump the blood around our bodies and keep the spring in our step, one name crops up almost unfailingly when the topic of radio is introduced: John Peel. At times it could feel as though Peel was a lone flag flying in a musical desert. However, it would be incorrect and unfair to not recognise the other beacons of hope, some on local BBC stations, others on independent stations.

Indeed, as the bands we knew and loved as alternative became increasingly popular and nudged the realms of the Top 40, flags even began to fly on - gasp - national BBC stations, as Paul Bennett recalls:

> It's 1991 and I'm 14 years old. My bedroom walls are adorned with posters of a female Australian singer/soap star. I have her album on 12" vinyl and hope that she will be my future wife … I should be so lucky. However, I start taking notice of a different type of music; songs by bands like EMF and Jesus Jones. These songs come on the radio and all of a sudden I feel more grown up and, dare I say it, cool.

 I give all my Kylie posters to my friend at school. Also a fan, he will continue following her career while I move on, into the world of indie music. Pocket money is saved and I purchase EMF's debut album *Schubert Dip*, I don't remember exactly where I buy it from: we had two record stores in my town (Reynold's Records and BigAl's), but it could quite easily also have been from the Co-op or Woolworths.

Schubert Dip becomes a permanent fixture on my Walkman during those long hot summer days when the memories I will have as an adult, of school holidays and the fun and games we had, will just be forming. It will not be long before I discover Blur, then Suede, and then Elastica and from that starting point I won't look back.

It would be churlish to suggest that it was just British radio stations spreading the word - many indie bands developed followings in Europe thanks to the efforts of other lone standard bearers, and American college radio stations had a similarly influential role across the Atlantic. Back closer to Britain, Dermot Greene began his journey with Ireland's own version of John Peel, Dave Fanning soundtracking revision for the all-important InterCert exams.

> "Bump." (needle hits the groove). Drum machine kicks in: "Duh Duh – Duh-Duh-Duh-Duh-Duh-Duh-Duh-Duh – Duh Duh." Then layers and layers of sound and over seven minutes of teenage angst to a dance beat with a killer Hooky bassline…
>
> I first heard New Order's 'Blue Monday' on the Dave Fanning show on RTE 2FM – Dave's show came on around 8pm during the week and he was our John Peel. This was the point where my musical taste started to transition from following mainstream electronic/new wave bands (Ultravox, Visage, Spandau Ballet, Human League and the like – all of who still bring back good

memories) to now seeking out more obscure music. It just sounded so ahead of anything mainstream at that time and looked so cool too.

I went and bought Blue Monday in our local Peter Graham's record shop in Mullingar (long since gone). I had to do a double-take that it was actually the right record – I mean, where was the band name and why did it look like a floppy disc? It was special because of that - here was a band who didn't put their name on the cover and sounded like nothing else I'd ever heard. No promotion, just word of mouth. I then bought *Power, Corruption and Lies* in Freebird Records, up the steep stairs on Dublin's Grafton Street, sometime in the summer of 1983 and still remember the shock of Blue Monday not actually being on the album – and come on, where was the next hit single?

For Dermot, like for so many of us, the next steps involved teenage-poverty-necessitated swapping of cassettes containing home-taped albums, singles and songs recorded off the radio and generally "investing a lot of time that should have been spent studying chasing down new obscure bands and recommending what was the next coolest band we should listen to … happy days indeed."

For those of us lucky enough to have access to his shows, however, the influence John Peel had on the musical tastes of so many of us was immeasurable. Whether it was the eclectic mix of song and style, the specially-recorded sessions with their often-superior versions of better known songs, the obscure 7" singles released on a homespun label by young idealists or the likely play of such favourites of his as the Fall, Half Man Half Biscuit and the Wedding Present, Peel was almost guaranteed to never disappoint. For William McAlpine it was the annual treat of the Festive Fifty that would provide the perfect introduction.

> There's not one specific record that I can think of that set me on the road to indieland. I'd been hovering round the edges of alternative music, peering over the fence by listening to my big sister's Smiths records, watching *Whistle Test* and *The Tube* and tuning in to Radio 1 in the evening, but not really with any great enthusiasm. I was an insecure, bookish teen and a bit of a loner away from school, comfortable in my own company – which was handy as I barely left the house.
>
> By December of 1985 I was - in the words of the Smiths song - 16, clumsy and shy. (Although unlike the

protagonist of 'Half A Person', I went to London and I ... stayed at my auntie's and went round all the museums and that with my mum and little sister). Then one night on Janice Long's show came the moment that would lead to one of the most protracted epiphanies in history, when John Peel popped into the studio to talk about what he was up to and started talking about something called the Festive 50, where listeners voted for their favourite songs of the year. I was intrigued and thought I'd give it a listen. I'd only heard his show once, when I'd fallen asleep during Janice and woken up in the middle of his show. I was bemused by it, I think. Angular, noisy guitar music interspersed with weirdness, including at one point a reggae version of the *Rawhide* theme. I hadn't tuned in again.

So on Monday 16th December 1985, a date which will live in infamy, I got myself ready with a C90 to record the first instalment on the family portable radio cassette player. (You know the one everyone had: knobs missing, aerial bent and the loading door-thing broken off.) I assume I listened until the actual countdown began about an hour an a quarter in, but I didn't record that so I don't know for sure. My memories of these five programmes are what I captured on Memorex - and they are still fixed in my mind to this day, when my ability to remember anything is getting Dory-like. The unfamiliar names I'd soon be following with interest (Shop Assistants, Primal Scream, James, That Petrol Emotion), ones I'd never hear from again (the Vibes, Rose of Avalanche), ones I'd heard of but would become obsessed by (Mary Chain, Cocteaus, Smiths, New Order, the Fall – oh, the Fall) and ones I'd steer clear of (the Cult, Sisters of Mercy – rum-tum-tum indeed, as Mr Peel said). And then there was the Wedding Present …

At number 15 was a song called 'Go Out and Get 'Em Boy', a frantic, rampaging, tinny, trebly mass of scrabbling guitars that threatens to collapse in on itself at various parts, all held together with a keening, urgent vocal and ending with what sounds like the guitar exploding. "Blimey!" as Peel said after it finished. I played all the tapes constantly over Christmas and into the New Year, but this was my favourite song, rewinding and replaying it endlessly as you do when you find something that just clicks with you. The weird thing was:

for some reason I didn't immediately start listening to Peel in January, but I obviously eventually decided to give it another go as I tuned in on the 26th February 1986. I know this as I've just Googled it, but I knew precisely what to search for, as it happened to be the night of the first-ever Wedding Present Peel session.

And that, dear reader, is how I ended up being glued to his show for the next three and a half years and how I discovered most of the artists I love. Even when I discovered drinking and going out I always made time at Christmas to tape the Festive 50 – how else was I going to know what to like? And since his death in 2004, I always have nagging doubts as to whether Peel would approve of what I'm listening to. As David Gedge sang in 'Go Out and Get 'Em Boy':

"Some things just don't ever go away, some things you know are just here to stay."

Lucky for William then that John Peel didn't take the advice of one of his listeners. In his biography of Peel, Michael Heatley describes how the DJ would "regularly complain that the listeners failed to keep up with the times … one of the more adventurous notions that one listener proposed was to list the top fifty tracks but broadcast numbers fifty-one to one hundred."[2] Who knows what path life could have taken with exposure to even more obscure artists and their songs?

---

[2] John Peel: a life in music, Michael Heatley, Michael O'Mara Books 2004

------ Fabulous Friend ------

At a time when we were without the immense and instant social networks with which we are now so familiar, as the second decade of the twenty first century draws to a close, radio could often seem like the friendliest voice our ears might encounter when it came to hearing alternative music. As Dermot notes in the previous chapter, the next step having heard something magical would be to share it amongst friends. Our acquaintances in those teenage years could be kind or be cruel, and finding a kindred spirit was not always plain sailing, especially for those who lived away from the big cities. When a fabulous friend was found, however, then musical adventures could begin, as Ian Fergie describes:

I was a little kid in the 1970s. We lived in a small mill village on the outskirts of Huddersfield, geographically and psychologically half-way between the *Last Of The Summer Wine* town and

Royston Vasey [as featured in the comedy series *The League Of Gentlemen*]. I have hazy memories of an idyllic childhood, where music was an integral part of most events. I was a big kid in the 1980s, and had a gradual realisation that there was life, and more importantly music, beyond the village's hymns and brass band marches. I have a vague feeling of this being a challenging decade, where music accompanied my progress through education. Most of the mills closed down.

The first record I bought with my own money was probably 'Get the Balance Right' by Depeche Mode. Not really indie ... (or is it?); I'm not sure why I bought it. The sleeve design intrigued me as much as the bouncy synth tune. I proudly showed the new purchase to my friend Pard, who was dismayed at my tastes and decided to introduce me to some 'alternative' music via the medium of the mix-tape. I wasn't convinced.

Like all good friends, Pard was undeterred and moved onto 'phase 2' of his musical re-education plan: he decided to take me out record shopping. Pard had older brothers, pretty cool older brothers, and seemed very streetwise to me. It was decided we should visit the new record shop in Huddersfield. Big Tree Records had recently opened and was somewhere in the middle of this parade of shops at the bottom of St. George's Square.

The shop entered an already crowded marketplace for record sellers in Huddersfield: Bostocks, Bradleys, Dead Wax, WH Smiths, Woolworths, Boots, Woods, two second-hand shops and some market traders. But, against stiff competition, it became an important place for my introduction to, and purchase of, indie music. My first impression was that it was a dark, cluttered, disorganised place. The owner was a very nice man, like a hippyish version of the shopkeeper in Mr Benn, and would later exchange errant purchases whilst pointing me in other directions. I sometimes wonder if it was all a clever ploy to broaden my musical horizons, I hope so. Pard liked the shop which would have been enough anyway, and on that first visit picked out a cassette album for me.

The Cocteau Twins' debut album *Garlands* was a complete revelation; I had never heard anything like it, and it blew my tiny mind. The hypnotic drum machine, drifting bass lines, pedal drenched guitar noise and dreamy, other-worldly voice captured my imagination and took on a mythical stature. Getting the album on cassette was doubly important. Firstly, I could listen on my newly acquired walkman whilst riding about. There's something really rhythmic about the mid-80s drum machines which is ideal for cycling and the album soundtracked many rides over the moors around Holme Moss. Secondly, the cassette version of *Garlands* included an early Cocteau's Peel session on the B side of the tape. This introduced me to a new world of late night radio and Peel's dry humour; my musical landscape was transformed.

The magic of the record shop is described beautifully by Nick Hornby in 'High Fidelity', one which many a customer would recognise, smelling "of stale smoke, damp and plastic dust covers" whilst the inside is "narrow and dingy and dirty and overcrowded".[3] In reality, quite the opposite of the store frequented by Mr. Benn. Indeed, there was to be no Mr.

---

[3] Nick Hornby, High Fidelity, Victor Gollancz 1995

Benn-type shopkeeper figure for Tracey Bowen, although a family friend made a pretty effective alternative…

> I can't really remember a time before I knew Mal. He was my Uncle Steve's friend and had been working for the family business since the tail end of the 1970s. I'd have been 8 or thereabouts when he joined the firm so he was there as far back as I can remember. Though I don't suppose I paid much attention to him until around 1984 when I was 13 and had taken to accompanying my parents to work in the school holidays (it beat hanging around the village we'd moved to a couple of years earlier where I had few friends).
>
> So I'd hang out in the workshop, making him cups of tea, listening to the radio, desperately trying to impress him. I thought he was basically the coolest person on the planet. He was post-punk perfection: bleached, dishevelled hair, combat trousers, scruffy t-shirt and a leather jacket. He looked like Budgie from the Banshees. Not that I knew who the Banshees were or what post-punk was at this point. But I would…

I'd been exposed to some alternative music already; my older brother was into Bauhaus and Soft Cell and Japan. Chart music was my mainstay though and I was a bit of a Duranie. To this end I'd entered a competition to win tickets to a Duran Duran gig at the Birmingham NEC (they needed some extra crowd footage for the live video *Arena* and arranged a gig for their hometown fans with tickets being given away via a newspaper competition). I'd excitedly told Mal and he promised that if I won tickets, he'd go to the concert with me. Well, it must have been fate because I did indeed win a pair of tickets. Mal was true to his word (and my mom was relieved I had an appropriate chaperone so she or dad didn't have to accompany me). I was over the moon. At this point, I was certain I was going to grow up and marry him one day (his beautiful wife a mere inconvenience in the mind of a 13-year-old with a crush).

Thus far in life, I'd seen Dean Friedman, the Hollies and the Kids from Fame in concert but Duran Duran was going to be the best thing ever. The strange thing was that when I got there I didn't want to storm to the front to fawn at Simon Le Bon's feet. I was happier to stay near the back with Mal. I strayed a short distance away from him during the show and even joined in with the screaming for a while but felt utterly ridiculous and soon decided that such childish teenybopper behaviour wasn't for me and returned to my much cooler companion. I told him afterwards that I hadn't really enjoyed the crowd and didn't think I was a Duranie any more. Thus began his mission to introduce me to a wider range of music.

He and his wife were huge Bowie fans so that was the starting point. He lent me *Ziggy Stardust* and *Diamond Dogs* and Lou Reed's *Transformer* for good measure. Much to his disappointment, I preferred the Lou Reed album (though I didn't fully understand most of the lyrics) and I never really got any further into Bowie. His next move - Siouxsie and the Banshees *Once Upon a Time / The Singles* - was more poppy. Just not the kind pop that I was used to at the time. It was dark and heady; punky and exciting. The next thing he tried me on was post-punk genius: the Teardrop Explodes albums *Kilimanjaro* and *Wilder*. I loved them instantly and wanted more. Only there wasn't any more Teardrops. However, Julian Cope did have his first solo album *World*

Shut Your Mouth out by this time which I promptly added to my wishlist and got for Christmas that year along with the Duran Duran's *Seven and the Ragged Tiger*, Paul Young's *No Parlez*, Everything But the Girl's *Eden* and Aztec Camera's *High Land, Hard Rain*. An odd mix indeed.

But that was the thing, I was still in a crossover phase. I'd outgrown Duran Duran but had subsequently discovered Frankie Goes to Hollywood. So Mal challenged me again and lent me the Zoo Records compilation *To The Shores of Lake Placid*. It filled in the backstory to so much of what he'd been telling me about. Holly Johnson's band Big In Japan, as well as really early Teardrop Explodes and Echo and the Bunnymen and other bands from the Liverpool scene that I'd never heard of before. There on the tracklist at the end of the *To The Shores of Lake Placid* tape, in my girlish handwriting still with circles over the i's instead of dots, was the reminder that he'd also lent me the Birthday Party EP *Mutiny! and Release The Bats* b/w 'Blast Off' 7" and the first Nick Cave and the Bad Seeds single 'In the Ghetto' b/w 'The Moon Is In The Gutter'. I was utterly blown away. The *Mutiny!* EP

had a lyric sheet and I carefully copied them out before returning the record to Mal. Like the Lou Reed album, I only partly understood the themes at my tender age but I devoured the words like some beautiful macabre poetry. This was definitely the kind of music I needed to be listening to.

It seemed whatever band I mentioned to him with a single in the charts, he'd come back with "well their early stuff was brilliant" and would promptly lend me more albums. A dig through a box of old tapes in the loft turned up the Cure's *Three Imaginary Boys* and *Seventeen Seconds*, Echo and the Bunnymen's *Heaven Up Here* and *Porcupine*, the Psychedelic Furs' *Forever Now* and *Mirror Moves* and the Smiths' *The Smiths*. Mal wasn't responsible for my first hearing the Smiths - I never missed *Top Of The Pops* so would have seen their debut in 1983 - but the first record of theirs I bought myself was *Hatful Of Hollow* having borrowed and taped the first album from Mal as soon as it came out. Through him I had access to records I couldn't afford to buy with my pocket money and cool stuff I'd missed by being a little too young to have heard it when it came out.

Some time in mid 1985, my dad and his brother had a massive fight and my Uncle Steve left the company. Mal left not long after. I was devastated. But by now I guess I was starting to forge my own identity and had found more ways of discovering my own kind of music: John Peel, *The Tube, The Old Grey Whistle Test*, music papers. I did pop in and visit Mal after he'd left. This of course was before the internet and mobile phones so I just turned up unannounced one Saturday hoping he'd be in. I'd missed him terribly but the visit felt awkward and I lost touch with him soon after. I suppose I'd grown out of my teenage crush and didn't need him any longer. That said, I'll always be grateful for his influence in broadening my tastes and steering me away from the mainstream. While most other kids of my age were still taping the Top 40 on a Sunday night, I was suddenly quite certain that I was 'indie' and bloody glad of it.

The pivotal point in Tracey's tale would appear to be her introduction to Bill Drummond's relatively short-lived but highly influential The Zoo project, which culminated in the album *To The Shores Of Lake Placid*. Drummond describes that album as "ridiculously lavish in its packaging. So much so that for every copy sold we lost more money. It was worth it."[4] Undoubtedly Tracey would agree. Meanwhile, her tale lends credence to the old saying that 'you can choose your friends but you can't choose your relatives'; happily for Alisdair Smith however, the bloodline was to have a very positive influence on his own musical tastes:

> As a child I was often left alone with my brother and my sister so, when they left for university, the high point of my existence was to wait for their periodic returns, washing and fancy student opinions in tow. The records of my sister are, thankfully, not relevant for this piece, but those of my brother are more so.

---

[4] Bill Drummond, 45, Abacus 2010

My first childhood memory of more or less anything is a massive Abba poster on my brother's wall, with them all wearing awful suits and panama hats set at jaunty angles, exuding a slightly seedy nightclub glamour mixed with extreme wealth and a shocking dress sense. But in the run up to him going away I can remember a change. I think the first of the records he bought was 'Birthday' by the Sugarcubes, which I didn't much like at the time; it felt alien and uncomfortable, but it had the sense of something that was other, that no one else knew about and as such it had an allure.

The records that he brought back from university had this in spades. Some were familiar to me after a fashion, Smiths LPs and such; others felt utterly foreign and remain so now; you don't see people digging Hugo Largo out much these days. My ten year old self outwardly dismissed them as a load of rubbish because they "didn't get in the charts". In reality, I thought they were great.

I wasn't going to admit this straight away though. Basically, I was nothing if not petty, and well prepared to argue a point if I knew it would irritate someone. I don't know if these new records made me 'feel' any different than my chart favourites; I was ten years old after all and I liked the pretty ones. To be honest, it's a bloody long time ago. But looking at these songs now, there is a grainy unfinishedness to them that I have always loved in music and I think that it must surely have started there.

I can't pin the change down to a single record because there wasn't one; there were many. The memories I have are of the clanging guitars and stuttering samples of 'Action Painting' by the Blue Aeroplanes, the mechanical stop/start riff and swooping baseline that ushers in 'Blue Eyed Pop' by the Sugarcubes (now fully rehabilitated) and the intoxicating thrill of the sweary breakdown (forbidden!) in Freak Scene by Dinosaur Jr. All these and more became staples, albums on tapes run off on a festeringly bad music system that played at something approaching 35 rpm and gave everything the faint whiff of Pinky and Perky in a wind tunnel.

This pattered along for a while. I would listen to my tapes of New Order, REM and Talking Heads, but as yet I was too young to even go to town by myself, let alone enter a record shop; these still held the menace of an as yet impenetrable adult world. However, I had started to read the Melody Maker, to keep up with what was going on in this secret universe. This was partly to make a connection with my then sainted brother but soon, once I'd become fully immersed, it became a world apart that he wouldn't have had the faintest idea about. I read about bands who I'd never heard of and some that I never would hear of again.

Over the next year or two, I became the kid in the My Bloody Valentine T-shirt two sizes too big who bought records that were five years beyond him. I spent long periods of time browsing in the various record shops in town, each with their own distinct attitudes and atmospheres, having earnest conversations about the new Bongwater LP with men three times my age who, though amused by the novelty, were always kind and never condescending.

Despite these connections, it still felt like this was my thing and mine alone. At school (big school now!) I would try and read Melody Maker in the house base, where I was regularly hassled for 'reading a newspaper' by kids who didn't know any better and cared less. I pretended to be annoyed and maybe I was, but I think that all I'd ever really wanted to do was stand out and at that I had truly succeeded, Though I loved many of the records I bought, there were a lot of them that I don't think I truly got the full measure of until several years later; I was basically just a twelve year old hipster. I was ahead of my time I suppose.

------ Running Order Squabble Fest ------

The logical pattern of musical discovery for those of us growing up in the pre-internet age was often something along the lines of hear a band, buy some records, go and watch them play live. [That wasn't always the case, mind you - the editor can still clearly recall the embarrassingly naive incredulity with which he responded to a school colleague saying he'd just been to see Nik Kershaw, on a school night to boot; surely people on TV didn't actually go and play concerts too?], as Peter Fraser's tale of indie discovery reveals:

> In 1988, aged 16 I only listened to heavy metal and rock music; Iron Maiden, the Cult, Guns and Roses and even a bit of Europe. Iron Maiden were playing Wembley Arena on their Seventh Sun of a Seventh Sun Tour. I had every album, an Eddie t shirt and a black leather bikers' jacket. Two things I did not have were my parent's permission (and credit card) and someone to go with. Minor details to the mind of a young eager fan.
>
> At school people were split into two groups: people who liked the Smiths and people who like Luther Vandross. I

mentioned to one of the Smiths brigade, who I knew also liked U2 and Queen, that I wanted to go to see Iron Maiden. He agreed to come along if I would go to see a band with him. He gave me a C60 cassette tape with the letters P.W.E.I. scrawled on in biro. I stuck it in my blazer pocket and agreed to his terms. Unbelievably, my mum handed over her credit card and I made the phone call to book tickets. In the end three of us went to Iron Maiden and I'm still really proud that that was my first ever gig. It was loud, entertaining and full of fireworks and stage production. My ears were still ringing in the morning but even then I felt that the whole thing was very corporate.

A few weeks later, February 1989, we set off for The Town and Country Club to watch Pop Will Eat Itself, with support from Nasty Rox Inc. and Yeah God! The C60 tape had been on hard rotation since I first played it. The album was *Box Frenzy* and it completely blew me away. The sound was so unique; it had the guitars that I loved and it also had samples, two singers, a sense of humour and a drum machine.

Approaching the venue in Kentish Town, I started to get a bit unnerved. The fans standing or sitting around in groups were drinking and smoking heavily and definitely looked alternative. I had decided to wear my Iron Maiden t shirt from the Wembley gig with my biker's jacket for which I was very grateful for. A group of scary looking blokes approached us. They had long dreaded hair, German army surplus jackets, black jeans and boots. They scoffed at my t shirt and said that kids weren't welcome. We ignored them and pushed on but I zipped up my jacket and it remained that way for the rest of the night.

Inside, the venue was dark and stuffy. We headed to the front and I was naively amazed that nobody else had had the same idea. By the end of the support bands' sets the front was packed and I was sweating profusely in my leather jacket. Suddenly it went quiet and dark. People started cheering then, unexpectedly, one of Vivaldi's *Four Seasons* blared out. I was stunned, I looked around and everyone was jumping up and down and screaming as Clint Mansell, Graham Crabb, Adam Mole and Richard March burst on to the stage. Clint was wearing black leather trousers, black boots and was bare chested, Graham had a mega phone and was crazily dancing around, Adam was climbing all over his keyboard, only Richard on bass guitar seemed normal. My head was spinning and soon I was too as I was bumped, shoved, shunted, jostled, elbowed and rammed around the venue. I fell over several times but each time a stranger's grinning face would look down and offer me a hand up.

Glasses were being thrown around the venue and after a few songs one of them hit Clint squarely in the face. He stopped the gig and launched into a vicious tirade. He threatened to rip of the head of the person who had thrown the glass. Needless to say no one offered to get on the stage. By the end of the gig I was drained. A combination of being terrified yet enthralled threatened to overwhelm me but I knew immediately that I would be a fan for life.

Peter's description of heading to the front of the venue to find relative acres of space will be familiar to many a gig-goer. The role of the support band can often be something of a poisoned chalice. In his review of the above gig for Melody Maker, Ian Gittins wrote: "NASTY ROX INC look like slobs but have a beat which cuts it. Their rock/hip hop amalgam makes all the right moves, yet never manages to excite. The dense beat bites deep, they all sport cowboy hats, yet still we yawn. They're very state-of-the-art, I'm sure. But well, really, so what?" [5] Harsh!

It is not unknown for a band to choose an act of very different style in order to make themselves sound better. Some venues have a laudable policy of offering support slots to up-and-coming local bands, but even then the value of exposure is potentially limited by the fact that, in reality, the audience has

---

[5] Melody Maker, 11 February 1989

only come to see one band, and it isn't the first band on. Sometimes, however, the gods of fate can smile kindly, as Jon Peachey's tale from August 1990 recounts:

A rare day trip out of East Anglia. It's a hot sunny early afternoon on a hill overlooking North London and a mildly inebriated chap saunters over, can of lager in hand, prods me firmly in the chest and loudly declares over his shoulder to anyone who will listen... "Bootleg!"

A few people smile as my accuser disappears back into the largely black clad throng and momentarily flushed with embarrassment I quickly weave my way back to my friends with the three ice creams I'd been despatched for. The T-shirt in question had taken a few days to make. At the time I had little money for official merchandise, let alone anything bootlegged, and the ticket for today (plus the standard chipping in for the petrol to get here) had pretty much wiped out what spare cash I had. The previous weekend I'd cycled into Bury St Edmunds and found a decent plain white T-shirt off the market and spent the rest of the week, using fabric paint left over from college days, to recreate my favourite LP cover.

That album was *Black And White* and the band were the Stranglers. I'd even added the band's name at a jaunty angle in that heavy red script to add a splash of colour. However, I couldn't get drummer Jet Black's brooding stare quite right and so in the end I left him with a somewhat comical, googly eyed expression. In fact I may as well have just stuck on a pair of tiny plastic googly eyes. No one would have noticed, no one would surely have looked at the t-shirt that closely.

This was Alexandra Palace and we were here to see the Stranglers, a band I'd adored since the latter days of upper school in the mid-1980's, after hearing a friend of a friend's copy of *Live X-Certs*. The gig was part of a weekend event celebrating the 5th birthday of the Town & Country Club and the 'Men in Black' were today's headliners. We'd have to sit through a few bands before they came on though.

As it turned out, this was to be singer/guitarist Hugh Cornwell's last appearance with the Stranglers although none of us knew this at the time: he quit the band right after leaving the stage that night. We would only find this out some months later when it was announced in a tiny article in the entertainment pages of a tabloid newspaper. Whilst it would be easy to look back upon the Ally Pally gig with a hint of sadness due to Hugh's rapid exit, this was actually far from the case. The band played a blistering set. In fact probably the best I'd seen them in the few short years I'd been following. Sonically they were amazing, with the band having recently been bolstered to a five piece with the addition of Vibrators guitarist John Ellis. More importantly for me however, were those bands we'd have to "sit through" first.

In order, those bands were: Vagabond Joy, the Family Cat, the Godfathers and That Petrol Emotion. Now, up to this point I'd not been to that many gigs and the majority of those were to see old punk and post-punk bands who occasionally drifted through Ipswich, Norwich or Cambridge (the three focal points which formed a sort of no-band, gig free Bermuda Triangle type zone in the middle of East Anglia at the time... and I pretty much lived slap bang in the middle). Lack of money and transport were big factors. This was a big day out for three musically-like-minded mates who'd bonded at school several years earlier ,and by god we were going to aurally and visually hoover up everything we could... and then try and remember in which side street we'd left the car.

"It was the Family Cat what done it, m'lud!" (and then the glowing embers of the Undertones, That Petrol Emotion, a couple of hours later.) There it is: if I had to pick one pivotal moment that skewered my heart musically then that day was it, on that hill in that building once used by the BBC. My music collection certainly wasn't non-indie at the time by a long shot. The Wedding Present, the Wolfhounds, Julian Cope, the Primitives, all *those* Manchester bands... all present and correct. John

Peel, Evening Sessions, *The Tube* ... all accounted for in some way or form, some still recorded on magnetic tape. However, I'd rarely experienced any of it live. Yes I'd heard of the Family Cat and That Petrol Emotion and probably read about them before in the usual weekly papers, but being in that same big room and listening and watching them play flicked a switch. They were amazing. I decided I was going to seek out more of this... I was going to investigate further, dig deeper ...

A defining moment in Jon's musical life then: discovering a band through the sheer pleasure of the live experience. Sometimes little quirks of fate can set us on a different path. Who knows: if the Family Cat's drummer had opted for the usual cobbling together of a drum kit from various sources instead of buying his very own, could there have been a whole different tale to tell? It is interesting to see things from the other side, how our pivotal moments fit into the working lives of those whose music we come to love. Kev Downing, the self-same drummer of the Family Cat, offers his recollections of that historical day exclusively for this book:

Aug 1990. The band had been playing for 18 months or so. Our first single was released (after we'd played less than 10 gigs) on July 31st 1989. From 89-90 we made some money playing lots of gigs and had now signed off. We had no choice after being reported to Dalston dole office by someone who went out of their way to furnish the DHSS with clippings from the NME. Called into a small room and presented with the press cuttings and copies of our records the guy accusing us of fraud declared himself a fan and had seen us a few weeks earlier.

Ally Pally was our biggest gig yet. It was decided that I should buy my own drum kit. Until then I had been using a kit cobbled together from bits donated by friends and kept from crawling across the stage by a couple of breeze blocks carried around with us. We sourced a decent second hand kit in Willesden and drove there in our transit to pick it up, the day before the Ally Pally show. The guy said it had belonged to Michael Jackson's drummer. (A pattern was emerging, Tim's VOX AC30 apparently belonged to Marc Bolan, although I've often wondered what Marc Bolan's amp was doing in a junk shop in Cornwall.) We bought the kit and drove straight to a warm up gig in Oxford. These first couple of years in the band were the most exciting: We were 5 friends, we played gigs, we rehearsed, but mostly we played table tennis, pitch and putt and backgammon in Clissold Park, and spent evenings at gigs and in Stoke Newington's pubs.

I walked to the gig that day, I could see Ally Pally from my house. There was no sound check, we went on and played. Lots of our friends were there. I was nervous, it was the first time we were filmed live and a camera man was so close to me I could smell him (tobacco, sweat and a curious whiff of damp dog). It was daylight, and I could see my friends in the audience. We turned our noses up at the Stranglers seedy onstage goings-on. (I seem to recall a woman dressed as a schoolgirl or something). Weeks later, a couple of us we drove to Birmingham to mix it for TV. I learned that when there is a camera close up of an instrument that instrument is turned up in the mix. It was around this time that we knew we didn't want to record an LP for £500 in 3 days again. We were using money from gigs to fund time in a decent studio. The next single was our last on our friend's Bad Girl label and the following year we signed to Dedicated/BMG.

For both Jon and the Family Cat there would be no more looking back.

------ Kill Your Television ------

For those of us for whom geography, finance, age or other factors (including, let's face it, a ridiculous disbelief that the artists we like might even play live and then, even if they did, that we might be able to get tickets) provided restrictions, there was always the television. In the United Kingdom it was nigh-on impossible to turn on the televisioon without seeing some band or other playing live in the 1980s. There was … well … let's see … Oh yes: *The Tube* and *Old Grey Whistle Test*. *The Chart Show* just played videos. For most artists *Top Of The Pops* was the bees knees, and although it gave the opportunity for bands to appear live, appearance is all it was as the bands generally mimed to backing tracks for bizarre royalty and contractual reasons.

Nevertheless, television could still provide an invaluable opportunity to convert the masses from mainstream mundanity to alternative adulation. Take the experience of Simon Smith for example:

> The Wonder Stuff, 'Don't let Me Down, Gently': *The Chart Show* certainly didn't let me down… It was like nothing I'd heard before. So catchy, a brilliant video and just seeing them on the telly - it was the first time I'd seen

a band and thought 'I want to be them / look like them'. Seeing as I was listening to Then Jerico and Thrashing Doves at the time I discovered the Stuffies, I have to say they well and truly changed my life!

I bought *Eight Legged Groove Machine* and then *Hup!* when it came out. The facts on the ITV Chart Show mentioned Jesus Jones and That Petrol Emotion so I bought their albums too. I became a massive indie kid, grew my hair long. I went to see Ride and Ned's Atomic Dustbin live and then about a year and a half later, in December '91, I saw The Stuffies live for the first time. Eat and Kingmaker supported - it was a crackin' gig! I listened to them every day for years and I still love them.

The power of four minutes of television exposure could be quite powerful. The impact on a band was, in theory at least, easily quantifiable as exposure led to sales led to increased revenues. The impact on the audience was perhaps even more significant, as they consumed songs and attached to them their life stories, as Miles Hunt noted in a 2018 interview with *Louder Than War.* Recalling a conversation about ownership of songs with Tom Robinson, he found his perception of financial ownership by publishers and emotional ownership by the writer challenged: "He said, 'No … it's your audience… they own them now These songs have been a partial soundtrack to their lives and your job now is that of the custodian.'"[6]

Whilst *The Chart Show* had the power to introduce those with more mainstream tastes to the hidden worlds of dance, rock and indie via their weekly showcasing of specialist charts, *Top Of The Pops* remained the holy grail for most artists, a magical stalwart of their own youth. The weekly primetime showing of the UK Top 40 and the gems contained within always had the power to capture the imagination of the willing viewer. Here's Neil Budd:

> 15th June 1989: R.E.M. Performing 'Orange Crush' on *Top Of The Pops*. It looked like nothing in the charts at the time. It sounded like nothing in the charts at the time. It was an amazing performance: a topless Michael Stipe bellowing the words into a megaphone. My record collection took a much better turn after this.

Top Of The Pops would come to the rescue of others, too. For the bands themselves an appearance could make a huge impact on sales of not only the single and accompanying album, but on the career prospects as a whole. Speaking to the Guardian in

---

[6] Interview with Paul Grace, Louder Than War, 4 November 2018

2004, The Bluetones' Mark Morriss described the consequences of television appearances: "Success happened so quickly. We were getting used to playing gigs of 250, so to go from that to playing to thousands was mindblowing. It felt awkward, like we crashed someone else's party. We didn't realise we'd be on that many front covers or TV programmes ... We went from one party to another. We had tables at the Brits next to Prince and Sheryl Crow."[7]

Whilst perhaps less illustrious, the Bluetones' appearance on *Top Of The Pops* could have quite an effect on the viewer as well as the performer, as Nicola Tyzack describes.

> Being asked how I first got into indie music is a tough question. As someone who has always liked all types of music, it's hard to know when this actually happened as I've never really put my taste into genres. I just listen to what I like. Plus, what is indie to me, might not necessarily be indie to you. It could be the time I first listened to 'Something For The Weekend' by the Divine Comedy. It could be when I went to see Ben Folds at Shepherds Bush Empire. Or it could just be when I first

---

[7] 'Britpop Casualties', The Guardian, 24 April 2014

heard *Expecting To Fly* by the Bluetones. Let's go for that one then. It was 1996....

I cannot remember when I first heard *Slight Return*, quite possibly on *Top Of The Pops*; it hit me for six. I was always into guitar music, but this was amazing. So fresh and new, I had to know who this band was.

I went into work and told my mate about this new band and his reply was "I knew you'd like them". I guess I must've been very predictable back then. Anyway, I bought the single, loved it and couldn't wait for their album to be released. It appeared on 12th February 1996. The band became my new favourite thing. Little did I know they would still be one of my most favourite things over twenty years later.

Expecting To Fly went to number one in the album chart (famously knocking *(What's The Story) Morning Glory?* by Oasis off the top spot for just one week, but what a week that was.) The singles released from the album - 'Bluetonic', 'Slight Return' and 'Cut Some Rug' - all hit top twenty in the UK charts; not bad going for a debut album.

My story of this album is one of companionship, loyalty and love. It's an album I have not stopped playing over those twenty years and it still remains one of my all-time favourites. It's always on my iPod and various playlists and it's the album I go to when I want to remember a time when I discovered something important in my music life or when I want to have my heart broken.

I'll admit, my attention to the band has drifted in and out over the years. I dipped out for a while after *Luxembourg*, then returned around *A Rough Outline*, but my love for that first album has never, ever waned. Twenty odd years is a long time to have something in your life, especially something that still feels like yesterday when you first heard it. And that's one of the many beautiful things about this album: it hasn't been touched by time. The songs still sound as good now as they did in 1996.

I can't claim to have had the same experience with this album as so many of the other fans I've talked to have, as it doesn't represent my first love or a relationship from that time. My workmate didn't like the band particularly so it doesn't remind me of him much, apart from the fact that he was clearly wrong on many levels. The love affair for me is with the music itself as it's kept me company all these years and I'm inexplicably bonded to it by time. I have other albums that I have loved very much and still listen to, but there's something about this one that makes it different.

It's now 2018 and I am 41. A lot has changed over the years, but one thing that has remained the same is that I still listen to this album and love it as much now as I did then. It may not be classed as indie to everyone and I know it's certainly not liked by everyone, but I don't think that really matters.

In time *Top Of The Pops* would see the value of real, live performances to the extent that these became the norm rather than an occasional treat. These days it is pleasing that the sight of somebody miming on television is a jarring oddity and that live performance - often with TV studio-necessitated creativity and adaptation - is what we come to expect. That said, the opportunity of a showcase on national television isn't always as immediately satisfying for the artist as it might be for the viewer. In his autobiography 'Set The Boy Free' Johnny Marr describes the reality as "quite an underwhelming experience for us all … stood in a deserted black box with zero atmosphere while we waited for the party to start."[8]

However, it can't be denied that a few minutes on the small screen could be the perfect chance to garner a new fan or a

---

[8] 'Set The Boy Free', Johnny Marr, Century 2016.

hundred. The value of a live performance on television in generating excitement for the consumer about new music is demonstrated perfectly in Paul Asplin's recollection of December 1983.

> I had a black and white television in my bedroom, it was one of those with a dial that you used to tune to one of the four TV stations available. The dial was extremely sensitive and in order to obtain a decent picture you had to move it slowly like you were attempting to open a safe. The first channel that came into view was BBC2, a band was playing live.

> "Wow!"

> What hit me first was the sound, intricate guitar lines, an aggressive drum sound and vocals of the like that I'd never heard before. This sound touched me like nothing previously: urgent, melodic and, to my fifteen year old ears, perfect. Absolutely perfect. It was though I'd been waiting all my life for this moment.

Looking closer at these black and white images I began to take it all in. Front and centre was the singer, wearing a baggy undone shirt with beads and a big quiff, he was cavorting round the petal-strewn stage, moving in a way that I'd never seen anyone else move before; arms and legs flailing in different directions.

On the right of the stage was just the coolest looking guitarist I'd ever seen. Looking quite small, with a beautiful black and white guitar, he stood glued to the stage, throwing just an occasional look over towards the singer. His hair reminded me of Peter Tork from the Monkees (I had no knowledge of Brian Jones back then), he wore a striped jumper, skinny jeans and on his guitar was effortlessly creating a jangling sound that I knew I'd never tire of listening to.

It wasn't just the band on stage that gripped my attention: the audience were waving flowers and throwing them towards the stage and the whole scene was one of adoration for this group who at this point I frustratingly knew nothing about.

There was one song in particular, it was slower than the others, the words seemed so poetic but at the same time so down to earth. Why wasn't anyone else writing lyrics like this?

"Reel around the fountain - slap me on the patio"

"Fifteen minutes with you - well I wouldn't say no"

I needed to know who these people were. I needed to know everything about them. Then, during a chaotic stage invasion the credits rolled. There it was, the information that I so urgently needed:

"The Smiths"

"Morrissey"

"Johnny Marr"

"Andy Rourke"

"Mike Joyce"

And my life changed forever.

Being on BBC2 and in 1983, the television show in question could only have been *The Old Grey Whistle Test*. As noted at the start of this chapter, in the early 1980s there were really only two shows that championed live music. Channel 4 had begun broadcasting a year previously, with its own champion of emerging music taking the form of *The Tube*. It would be this show that would provide Ben Vendetta with his own escape from the mainstream, a band described by Alan McGee as "just totally depressing people ... [who] would just moan the whole time"[9].

I grew up in Ann Arbor, Michigan, the birthplace of Iggy Pop and a stone's throw away from Detroit and Motown Records. As a kid I loved hard rock and soul in equal measures. My first real concert was Rick James in 1982 when I was just seventeen. At this stage in my life, I wouldn't have called myself a music fan, but like most kids of my generation, I had a decent record collection; we didn't have the competition from video games and the internet that today's kids experience.

Around this time, I started to become enchanted with post-punk/alternative artists via MTV, including the Psychedelic Furs, Echo and the Bunnymen, and U2. My transformation from fan to music obsessive transpired while I was at University. When I started at the University of Michigan in 1983 my main goal was to make the varsity cross country team, but those plans capsized within months as I tried, without success, to

---

[9] 'Creation Stories', Alan McGee, Pan 2014

balance out long distance running, keeping up with my classes, and partying like a rock star. In high school I would drink occasionally on the weekends, but without parental supervision things quickly got out of control. I ended up quitting the team, later even getting hospitalized for a week with pancreatitis. I had become so depressed that I ended up seeing a shrink and got prescribed Valium. I certainly didn't mind that part! My second year was a blur. It probably sounds cliched, but I felt like I didn't belong and was looking for an exit strategy. Music and rock 'n' roll fashion started to take over my life as I bought every British magazine I could get my hands on and started to copy the way my favorite bands dressed.

On a whim, I decided to apply for two programs in England: University of Essex and York University, just days before applications were due. I ended up getting accepted at both schools, choosing Essex because of its closer proximity to London. Essex was a completely different world to Michigan. The students were much more politically active, and I felt like I didn't have to search so hard to find kindred spirits.

It was during my first month at Essex that I heard the band that would change the course of my life, the Jesus and Mary Chain. I was watching *The Tube* on a small television in a friend's room in our tower flat when the Mary Chain appeared into my life. I was struck by how cool they looked. Head-to-toe in black, except for the drummer Bobby Gillespie who was sporting a red roll neck jumper with leather trousers. 'Just Like Honey' floored me. The sixties girl group drum sound blending in with scuzzy guitars, the dark melodies, and the gorgeous backing vocals. It was like the perfect Motown hit from an apocalyptic parallel universe.

Psychocandy came out the next month. I bought the album on the day it was released, and it has remained my all-time favorite. I vividly remember stopping at the campus shop that day to buy copies of the NME and Melody Maker. The Mary Chain were on the cover of both. I decided to skip my lecture and take the short bus journey to Andy's Records in Colchester to buy the album on cassette to play on my cheap boombox I bought when I arrived.

Psychocandy became the soundtrack to my year abroad. I bought every magazine I could that had articles about the Jesus and Mary Chain, even cutting and styling my hair into a spiky mess as a homage to the Reid brothers. My best friend was another like-minded American named Marc. He arrived on campus in January. We met at a campus disco a few days after he landed in London; the two American dudes with pierced ears. I told him about *Psychocandy*, which hadn't come out in America yet, and he was desperate to hear it. We ended up going back to my room and playing my cassette and drinking whiskey out of a bottle that I had on my shelf and became friends for life. Marc got me into a lot of great music. He had a cassette of some previously unreleased Velvet Underground tunes that I had never heard, and we saw countless shows together.

More than any other band, the Jesus and Mary Chain changed my life for the better. Without the Mary Chain and that fateful encounter with 'Just Like Honey' on a grainy TV in a tower flat, I don't think I would have dived so deep into music and become a music writer, indie record label owner, and, currently, the author of three rock 'n' roll themed novels. I sign copies of my books with the inscription "rock 'n' roll saves lives" because the Jesus and Mary Chain saved mine.

------ A Trip Out ------

One of the joys of growing up - although it might not always feel like it at the time - is learning to be away from the comfort of home. Sometimes it can prove to be quite a baptism of fire, as mattress is swapped for farmers field, brick for canvass, *Coronation Street* for a badly-filmed drama in an unfamiliar language… So dramatic are the changes to the norm that is perhaps only to be expected that the soundtrack accompanying them can have similar life-defining influence. For Adele Pascale it was the Girl Guides who provided the necessary change of environment:

"Aaaaaalllll the people, so many people, and they aaaaalllll go hand in hand, hand in hand through their… PARKLIFE!!"
And as I stood there, tentatively sipping contraband vodka from a plastic bottle, I could feel a shift in my life as I knew it.

My life in music had begun with my dad's influences but, as I approached secondary school, I started to find my own feet with what I liked. By the time I was 14 I was an alternative kinda gal. I stomped around in my DM's (in the days when they were boots and not weird men trying to hit on you) paired with tea dresses or oversized checked shirts and baggy jeans stolen from my Dad. I listened to Nirvana, Green Day, Offspring, Hole, REM. If my hair wasn't so stupidly black I'm sure I'd have become a Courtney Love Style dirty blonde....

And then I went to Girl Guide Canoe Camp... Yeah yeah, it sounds lame, but my mum was - and still is - the leader. In fact there's a good chance I'm still in the Guides - she wouldn't let me leave.

The older girls there introduced me to boys, booze and most importantly Blur although I didn't realise who they were at the time. I copied them as they sang along by the campfire. I knew the words - well the chorus - before I had even heard the song, but there was something about that cockney style knees up round the fire (and contraband vodka and the promise of seeing a Scouts woggle no doubt) that really appealed to me. I managed to find out what the song was called and I used my pocket money to buy the tape. I remember it was from Our Price.

I remember it was a Tuesday because we were on 'day release' from school and I was doing a t-shirt printing course in town. I remember that my other purchase that day were some checked trousers from TopShop. I remember that green cover with the pint of beer so vividly. I went home and played it. Then I played it some more and my journey into Britpop was well and truly underway.

As I became a surly teenager still stuck in the Girl Guides I saw Damon perform on *Top of the Pops* in a Guides t shirt and secretly hoped that maybe I was a little bit cool after all …

The cool of canvass is swapped for the slightly more exotic hard walls of a youth hostel for Mark Whitworth in his tale of indie discovery although, it must be noted, the introduction to his story does suggest being somewhat closer to the indie front line than the general 'first steps' theme ...

It's late 1990 and yours truly is in the sixth form in Northwich, Cheshire, the hometown of Tim Burgess. The Charlatans' debut album, *Some Friendly*, had shot to number one a few weeks before, and on that occasion some fellow students had cajoled me into going along to their manager Steve Harrison's record shop, Omega Music, in the town centre for a celebratory beverage. To be honest at that time I'd barely heard of the Charlatans, but the idea of a glass or two of champagne on my dinner hour was too good to turn down, despite the subsequent haze through which I experienced the afternoon's French classes.

Until I started the sixth form, my musical taste was, looking back now, pretty bland to be honest. I'm sure we all liked bands/artists back then who we cringe about now, but really I'd just fallen in line with the well-worn treadmill of Smash Hits readers and Radio 1 listeners of my generation, and had a wall full of posters of Stock/Aitken/Waterman artistes and a record box mainly full of Erasure, late 80s *Now That's What I Call Music* albums and novelty singles (the theme from *Supergran* and 'Fedora (I'll Be Your Dawg)' from the Kia-Ora advert, anyone?). Spike Island was about 30 minutes' walk from my mum and dad's house, but I didn't even find out about the legendary Roses gig until months later. There hadn't been any sort of music scene in my secondary school and the whole thing had completely passed me by.

So, having partaken of the Charlatans' celebratory bubbly, I felt the least I could do was give their album a listen. I asked one of the lads I'd gone along with to do me a copy – flagrantly disregarding the dire warnings about home taping killing music – and I really liked what I heard. I loved the drumbeats, the fantastic keyboard and the winsome vocals (although even now I've no idea what some of the lyrics are). This was the way forward, I thought – I had to get hold of some more stuff like this.

A couple of months later in February 1991, and the sixth form German class headed off for a week in a youth hostel in Heidelberg. I took along a little cassette player and a few tapes, the Charlatans one and I can't remember which others. I told a couple of lads I'd be taking my player and asked them to bring some tapes with them. One lad brought 2 tapes – The Stone Roses' eponymous classic, and the Inspiral Carpets' debut album *Life*. I'd already recently heard the Roses album and had become a huge fan, but the Inspirals were completely new to me at this point – I'm not even sure if I'd heard the name before.

Anyway, the tape duly went on and for the first 30 seconds or so I remember thinking "What the hell is this?" If you know the album, you'll know I'm referring to the slightly pyschedelic synth/brass intro to 'Real Thing'. Then ... BOOM ... a crash of guitars, drums and keyboards; I'd genuinely never heard anything like it. The Charlatans had their Hammond – they utilised it extremely well but it was a well-known sound. However, the Inspirals' Farfisa (I found this out years later) was something else altogether. I was hooked straight away and although there wasn't, and isn't, a poor track on it, I was particularly struck by 'Song For A Family', 'This Is How It Feels', 'Directing Traffik', 'She Comes In The Fall' and 'Sackville'.

As soon as I got back from Germany, I went to our local library and borrowed a vinyl copy of *Life*. (Only 25 years later and this already sounds as anachronistic as the concept of phlogiston or the aether). I taped a copy and played it constantly on the hour-long bus journey to and from college, learning every word, note and beat. Before long one of the lads said to me: "You know they've done loads of other stuff, don't you?" Needless to say I had no idea. He duly compiled a tape for me containing loads of pre-*Life* and non-album tracks and B-sides such as 'Joe', 'Find Out Why', 'Commercial Rain' and the 'Island Head' EP. Some of these remain my all-time favourite songs to this day.

Having just discovered this amazing band, you can imagine my delight when their second album *The Beast Inside* was released just a few weeks later. Somewhat darker lyrically and musically than its fast-paced garage-orientated predecessor, tracks such as 'Born Yesterday', 'Grip', 'Mermaid' and the brooding 13-minute epic 'Further Away' were right up there with anything I had heard so far.

By this time, I was picking up stuff by other bands who were being grouped together under the burgeoning 'Madchester' umbrella – Happy Mondays, Northside, non-album Roses stuff, etc. The Inspirals remained my first love however, and in February 1992 myself and a mate went to see them at what was my first ever gig, at the Royal Court in Liverpool. To say I was excited is a massive understatement. The Inspirals were absolutely magnificent – everything I'd hoped for and much more. They played pretty much everything I'd been wanting to hear, plus a few tasters from their forthcoming album *Revenge of the Goldfish*.

So I have a lot to thank Sir John Deane's College in Northwich and that trip away for. If I hadn't had this musical epiphany there, who knows what I might have ended up listening to for the rest of my life, where these musical choices would have taken me, or who I'd end up falling in love with because of them...

------ Sleeping With The N.M.E. ------

One by one the stalwarts of the music press have disappeared from the stands of the local newsagent; Record Mirror, Smash Hits, Sounds, Number One, Melody Maker, Select, NME … The digital age has seen a huge change in not only how we listen to music but how we find out about it. However, there can be no denying the ability of music journalists to make and break bands. The 'build them up to knock them down' accusations have been flung at music magazines and papers for as long as they have existed; to some extent there may be some degree of truth in them. Nevertheless a band or artist has to have had a fair degree of positive coverage in the first place to be in a position to be at risk of the latter and it is ultimately up to us as collective listeners to decide where their career heads next.

For many of us, the pop-focussed Smash Hits was invariably our first taste of music journalism, but credit was always due to the magazine for drawing attention to artists whose existence did not -at that stage at least - trouble the Top 40. Russell Barker was one of many who were able to take advantage of this:

There was an epiphany, a sun breaking through the clouds moment. But not just yet. First there was a false start.

As the Eighties began I first met someone who would become a long-time friend, and still is to this day. He came to our small town from the outskirts of Birmingham with a handful of 2 Tone records. We crowded round another friend's little record player and were suitably impressed. But then my head was turned by other people from school and the popularity of the new romantics, so I drifted away to that; always a sucker for an insanely catchy melody.

I used to watch *Top Of The Pops* every week and also got Smash Hits too. I mean, that's what everyone else did at school, so why not. It meant I could join in the conversations, or would have done if I wasn't so painfully shy. And it was this shyness and feeling that, despite my best efforts to fit in, I was actually quite different to most of my schoolmates, which drew me towards Billy Bragg. There had been an article in Smash Hits talking about how he had busked with a backpack with speakers attached in his early days. It piqued my interest a little, seeing someone who didn't look like he should be in the pages of that magazine.

The key moment though occurred on 21st March 1985 (don't worry, I haven't remembered this, I did have to look it up). Amid the usual suspects, Nik Kershaw, Phil Collins, the Power Station and Loose Ends, there he was, the boy with the big nose, electric guitar and interesting voice singing 'Between The Wars'. To say I was blown away would be an understatement. I couldn't get my head round what was happening, that stark jarring tune, harsh vocals and lyrics that meant something. This was the first occasion of hearing a song and going away to try and understand what the artist was singing about.

I needed to get hold of this single. More excitement

ensued on discovering the record was an EP that was "Pay no more than £1.25": three more tracks to delve into at a bargain price. It's no understatement that having 'Which Side Are You On?', 'World Turned Upside Down' and 'It Says Here' on that record as well as 'Between The Wars' shaped me as a person. It made me think and be more compassionate towards others. Who could hear those songs and not become a socialist?

The baptism led to exploring the margins more deeply. Further down the newsagent shelves from Smash Hits lay the weekly inkies. Even at 50p, I couldn't afford them all every week, but always bought one, usually NME or Melody Maker. Every now and again they would have a free record or tape on the cover, which created many a dilemma and sometimes mean having to stretch to afford more than one so as not to miss out. Via the weeklies I was lead to Peel and Janice Long and from that there was no turning back. Tapes were filled, but records bought when money allowed.

By November 1985 this had all progressed to gigs, with some friends and I seeing the Cult at Birmingham Odeon (with the assistance of transport from our dads of course). A month later and the opportunity would present itself to see Bragg at the same venue. As if to accentuate the eclectic nature of this alternative music I was now discovering, the support acts were the Hank Wangford Band and the Frank Chickens.

As an afterword, you know how they say to never meet your heroes? Well, it's not always true. In 2015, 30 years after that first encounter with his music, I met Bragg for the first time, and again less than a year later. Both times he was nothing less than delightful.

Good old Smash Hits! Mind you, had he read the magazine's review of 'Between The Wars' Russell might have been less inclined to pay attention when Bragg appeared on the television: "Oh dear. I hate this man and his music" began the review before continuing: "It's got the same monotonous tune all the way through and he can't sing to save his life. Why don't you just leave the music business, Billy?" In fairness, the review was written by a guest reviewer, twelve-year old

Marshall O'Leary.[10] That said, sometimes the press that mattered was even less obvious than a teen-orientated fortnightly, and it will be of some relief to the editors of in-store magazines to see, in this final tale from Rob Morgan, that their endeavours were not wasted. Even if it was just a stepping stone to the more 'traditional' music press.

> 1983 was my musical epiphany. A door to a world of music was opened ajar slightly by my Christmas 1982 present of a Sanyo music centre; that door was opened more by the discovery of Radio Luxembourg a month or so later and then truly kicked in by the launch of an HMV shop in Cardiff, the nearest big city, in April 1983. Now I wasn't just taping songs off the radio, I had the ability to buy them. Life changing? Ask my bank balance: it's never been the same since.
>
> Every spare penny of pocket money was saved for the fortnightly trip to Cardiff for new records. I didn't know much about music but I knew what I liked, so it was OMD, Freur, Heaven 17, A Flock Of Seagulls, Devo: electronic pop was definitely my thing. Oh yeah, I was 13

---

[10] Smash Hits, 14 March 1985. The review was sourced from likepunkneverhappened.blogspot.com, a treasure-trove of *Smash Hits* content.

going on 14, that is very important. It was important then, and important now I know that that is the age when what you surround yourself with become most influential on you.

HMV had a monthly newspaper called More Music, filled with interviews, news, album reviews and some charts. This was my first exposure to the music press and those charts gave me a glimpse of another world, for there was an indie chart. I had no idea what an 'indie' was and the records and bands listed seemed to be from another universe. The Fall. Cocteau Twins. the Birthday Party. Southern Death Cult. The only name I recognised on the chart was New Order, with 'Blue Monday'. I'd loved that song but could never find it in HMV. I hadn't twigged that the mostly black twelve inch single which looked like the floppy discs I used on the BBC Micros in school was the elusive seven minute wonder. As for the album with a painting of flowers on it ... no idea. It sat in the rack, beautiful yet aloof, not yielding any of its secrets.

Spring turned to summer turned to autumn 1983. 'Blue Monday' was back in the charts, joined by 'Love Will

Tear Us Apart' by Joy Division. At this point I had no idea the two bands were connected, but I loved both songs. Meanwhile my beloved futurist chart on Radio Luxembourg was cancelled, so now what was I going to listen to at night? I lay in bed, headphones on and spun the dial. I recognised the voice of John Peel from *Top Of The Pops*, and he was introducing music I didn't understand. There was the Fall with 'Eat Y'self Fitter', Microdisney were in session and 'Sleepless' caught my attention enough to get me to write it in my diary. There was also the Smiths - he played the New York dance mix of 'This Charming Man' which I preferred to the version on the radio I knew. I occasionally tuned into Peel, I certainly heard parts of the 1983 Festive Fifty, and that made an impression too. But by this stage I still had not bought any 'indie' records.

Finally in the early Spring of 1984 something clicked. I started reading Melody Maker, something I would continue until it stopped many years later. This opened my eyes to what was beyond the charts, records by bands I'd never heard of on labels with exotic names like Mute, 4AD, Factory, Cherry Red. Meanwhile the 120 issue partwork History Of Rock my father collected was reaching its conclusion, and one of the last issues featured Joy Division and New Order. Suddenly the link was made, and it showed pictures of New Order record sleeves as the band by now were evidently quite shy of cameras, it seemed. Now I understood a little more of the Joy Division/New Order story, I wanted to hear the music. After checking out what details I could find on the Joy Division albums I decided that *Still* was the best value for money: a double album for £3.99 (a special offer). I loved the sleeve, the blankness of the grey cardboard, the way the inner sleeves fitted into the outer sleeve, the minimal credits. And more than anything I loved the music.

I suppose I ought to get this out of the way now.... I was 14, I was moody and misunderstood, rowing with my parents and brother and teachers and friends, bullied in school, rolling from one unrequited crush to the next while feverishly noting down every slight glimpse of the unrequited one in my diary. On the one hand that's typical teenager fare, on the other hand the untold misery and secret depressions and terrible thoughts were signs of

Asperger's Syndrome which would go undiagnosed for another few decades. But in my desperate search for something or someone which would know how I felt and reflect my confusion with life and how to live it, I thought Joy Division would offer some solace. And yes I'll admit it, there was the tragic story of Ian Curtis which entranced me - it was also a hint to everyone else around me that I meant it, man. This was deep stuff, folks. I'm listening to Joy Division, take me seriously. (Oh come on, I was fourteen remember.)

Did *Still* disappoint? Hell no. It was everything I hoped for. The studio songs were mostly fantastic, the live songs gave me an idea of what the rest of their catalogue would sound like, and the version of 'Sister Ray' would be played frequently at my Lou Reed worshipping brother to annoy him. The songs which stood out to me were 'The Only Mistake', 'Dead Souls' and 'Isolation'. Was it the words or the music which captured me? Both really; the music built up and up relentlessly, and the vocals had a passion and pain within them which spoke to me. Did it help me understand myself? No not really. The opening line of 'Disorder' (on the live album) struck me as pertinent - "I've been waiting for a guide to come and take me by the hand". If Ian Curtis felt like that, what hope was there for me? Even if it did offer cold comfort for my emotional well-being, it certainly made me want to hear more.

A week or so later I bought *Power, Corruption and Lies* and that blew my mind more than *Still*. Here was electronic pop, but with guitars and bass and proper drums, all mangled and merged into sleek, thoughtful, intelligent, funny, sad dance music. I marvelled at the packaging, at the label, at the music and at the lyrics. I finally had a record with a swear word on it, and just as my brother would delight in playing 'Bodies' by the Sex Pistols at top volume, I would respond with 'Your Silent Face', turning up the volume for the final line of the lyric. I loved the music, the lyrics, the Factory packaging, everything about the records appealed to me. I was smitten.

------ Outro ------

Whichever generation we may belong to, it is safe to say that in our early teens much is expected of us: which subjects to take at school, whether to follow an academic or a vocational path to achieve the career we have already decided we want to spend the rest of our lives working in, to demonstrate the independence and maturity those older than others have spent years trying (and often failing) to achieve. All we actually want to think about is what music, clothes and hairstyles will make us more attractive to the people we want to be emotionally involved with, what exactly this thing called 'emotion' is, and why our bodies are growing hairs in places they have never grown before.

It seems fair to say that by the time the generation born between, say, 1965 and 1979 has begun its fifth decade, most of its participants will have fallen in and out of love with several people, and had a number of jobs not all within the same field of employment. However the contributors have demonstrated in these pages that their love for certain bands - 'indie' to them and therefore likewise to us - has been a constant throughout their lives. Television programmes, DJs, newspapers and magazines, friends and family have all helped set lifestyles and lives in particular directions, but most of all it has been the artists themselves who have helped us make the great leap forwards from the children we were to the adults we are.

------ Title Credits ------

'It Began On Radio' is performed by The Upper Room and can be found on their 2006 long player *Other People's Problems* released on Columbia Records. The contributors to this chapter are Paul Bennett, Dermot Greene and William McAlpine. Illustrative photographs were provided by Paul and have been reproduced with his kind permission.

'Fabulous Friend' is performed by the Field Mice and can be found on the b-side to the single Emma's House, released on Sarah Records in 1988. Sharing their stories in this chapter are Ian Fergie, Tracey Bowen and Alisdair Smith. Ian would like to dedicate his contribution to the memory of his son, noting "I wrote the piece during last year's hot summer when my son was very ill. It's basically me remembering nice bits of my life at his age and inspired by grief for a lost child. So I have included a photo of me & Peter together from 29th May 2017 when Huddersfield got promoted to the Premier League." Further illustrative photographs were provided by Tracey and have been reproduced with her kind permission.

'Running Order Squabble Fest' can be found on the album *This Leaden Pall* by Half Man Half Biscuit. It was released in 1993 on Probe Plus. Contributions in this chapter have been made by Peter Fraser and Jon Peachey, along with Kevin Downing to whom we are extremely grateful for providing an alternative take on a momentous day. Illustrative photographs were provided by Jon and have been reproduced with his kind permission.

'Kill Your Television' was a single released by Ned's Atomic Dustbin in 1990 on Chapter 22. Simon Smith, Neil Budd, Nicola Tyzack, Paul Asplin, and Ben Vendetta all provided their thoughts and musings on the importance of television on their discovery of music. In this chapter thanks are due to Nicola for allowing us to reproduce her photograph to illustrate the stories.

'A Trip Out' is written and performed by British Sea Power and resides on their 2007 album *Do You Like Rock Music?*, released on Rough Trade Records. Adele Pascale and Mark Whitworth are the contributing writers for this chapter, with illustrative photographs being kindly provided by Adele.

'Sleeping With The N.M.E.' is the title of the b-side to a 1992 single sponsored by that self-same music publication, namely Manic Street Preachers' interpretation of 'The Theme From M*A*S*H*' (also backed with the Fatima Mansions' take on the Bryan Adams track 'Everything I Do (I Do It For You)' on Columbia. Providing their memories for this chapter are Rob Morgan and Russell Barker, who also kindly allowed us to reproduce his photograph.